Anglican-Methodist Conversations

Summary and exposition of the official report:

Conversations between the Church of England and the Methodist Church

---

by HAROLD ROBERTS

THE EPWORTH PRESS

AND

THE CHURCH INFORMATION OFFICE

First published in 1963

© The Epworth Press 1963

Book Steward

FRANK H. CUMBERS

and the Central Board of Finance
of the Church of England

Printed in Great Britain
by Bookprint Limited
Kingswood, Surrey

Contents

Foreword

As joint chairman with Dr Roberts of the Anglican-Methodist Conversations, I gladly commend this summary and exposition of the Report. I hope it will be widely used by members of the Church of England as a basis of their own discussions, and also by local groups of Anglicans and Methodists who are thinking and praying together about the proposals.

HARRY OXON

Introduction

The following pages are intended to serve as an exposition of 'Conversations between the Church of England and the Methodist Church' (Church Information Office and the Epworth Press). Throughout, the needs of Study Groups have been kept in view. While it is hoped that the exposition may prove of some use to Anglicans and Methodists, special attention is directed to issues that affect Methodists more acutely than Anglicans. An attempt has been made to summarize the section in the Report entitled: A Dissentient View. Professor C. K. Barrett, one of the four signatories of the section, was asked to provide a summary lest an injustice should be done to the important views there expressed. He felt, however, that the text was in itself a summary and that, in any case, its presentation might be left to me. As far as possible, I have used the words of the text as it appears in the Report.

In some parishes and circuits, arrangements have already been made for meetings of groups. Where in Methodism no plans have yet been made, some guidance may be desired.

Unless Conference of 1964 revises the length of the period for discussion, the Report will be submitted to Conference 1965 for judgement. In that case discussions should be planned with that date in view.

It is hoped that no attempt will be made to invite the judgement of Quarterly Meetings and Synods until sufficient time has been allowed for the consideration of the Report. Further, it is desirable that the Report should be submitted, if possible, to all the Quarterly Meetings and Synods at approximately the same time so as to secure an independent judgement in each Circuit and District.

The suggestion is therefore made that the Report should come before the Quarterly Meetings December 1964 and the May Synods May 1965.

It should be noted that it is the Report itself in an unamended form that is to be presented to Quarterly Meetings, Synods and the Conference. The judgement to be given is to be on the main proposals of the Report as summarized on p. 27 of the present exposition. The question to be answered is whether these proposals as they stand are approved as the way forward to closer relations between the Church of England and the Methodist Church.

In Quarterly Meetings and Synods, it is possible that various amendments or modifications will be suggested. Doubtless a similar situation will arise in the Church of England.

It would be an advantage if in each Synod there were a small consultative committee to which such amendments could be sent, particularly if it was desired that any from Quarterly Meetings should be specially represented at the Synod. No doubt many amendments would be identical in substance and it would simplify the procedure in Synods if they could be reviewed by such a committee so that the mind of the Circuits could be fairly expressed.

The Synods might desire to send amendments to Conference for consideration. These amendments might be collated by the Synod consultative committee and sent to a Connexional Consultative or Continuation Committee representing different interests. The latter Committee should prepare the amendments for inclusion in the Conference Agenda. Again, no doubt there will be considerable duplication which can be avoided by editorial supervision. Reference could be made to the various Circuits or Synods that had forwarded similar amendments to those which are printed.

It must, however, be made clear that the main proposals must first be submitted to the judgement of Conference, and an answer given to the question: 'Do the proposals indicate the way forward?' If Conference gives its approval and if the same verdict is given by the Convocations of Canterbury and York, it will be necessary to appoint a negotiating committee representing the two Churches. That committee would need to examine with great care among other things the various amendments that had been received from Church courts. It would then report back to Conference and the Convocations, and seek approval of any recommendation it might desire to make.

While there must be no unnecessary delay in the quest for closer relations, it is clear that the Churches must not be stampeded into decisions or become victims of an unduly rigid time-table.

One further point may call for comment and it relates to the organization of groups. There is much to be said for the calling of a preliminary meeting in each District in the autumn at which the Report could be introduced and suggestions made about the most effective methods of group study, particularly in certain areas which present unusual difficulties. Members of the committee that was responsible for the Report would doubtless be willing to speak at such a gathering if desired.

In regard to Circuit groups, a leader should be appointed and a secretary whose responsibility it would be to convene the meeting and act as scribe. Meetings should be held about once a month and the section of the Report under consideration should, where possible, be introduced by a group member. It may be that in some Circuits the attendance would be too large for the purposes of a single group. In that case, the members could divide into small groups and come together at the close for an open session.

Every effort should be made to establish contact with Anglican groups. Even where joint meetings are not practicable, an endeavour should be made to secure Anglican speakers from time to time to speak to the Methodist groups. The need for joint meetings for prayer and study cannot be too strongly emphasized.

The Report should provide an opportunity not only to discuss proposals for closer relations but to consider afresh the mission of the Church to the world.

* * * *

In conjunction with the Report, the Interim Statement should be studied, since it deals more fully with some of the theological issues raised in the Conversations. *Anglicans and Methodists Talk Together*, written in the course of the Conversations by members of the Committee, will also be found most useful.

I have to thank my colleague, Dr Marcus Ward, for his kindness in reading the proofs and making helpful suggestions.

HAROLD ROBERTS

A*

1. Why Christian Unity Matters

A short time ago at a meeting about the Anglican-Methodist conversations a lady put a seemingly innocent question to the speaker.
She wanted to know why we should be constantly exhorted to work
for the union of the Churches. Could she and others who were similarly
perplexed be told why Christian unity was so important? Here then
are reasons why the visible unity of the Church is of supreme concern
to all Christians.

1. The Church in the New Testament is one.

(*a*) While the Christian Church was founded on earth by Jesus in the very
act of drawing his disciples to Himself, it became conscious of itself as a
community on the day of Pentecost following the Cross and Resurrection.
Those who gathered in the Upper Room in obedience to Christ became
united to one another through their union with Him. 'They continued
steadfastly in the apostles' teaching and fellowship, in the breaking of
bread and the prayers' (Acts 2: 42). The word translated 'fellowship' does
not mean an organization or a spiritual atmosphere. It was a common
life that resulted from sharing in the new life in the Spirit that came with
Jesus Christ. And it expressed itself among those early Christians in
bearing each other's burdens and in the unmistakable marks of unity
(cf. 2: 44–5; 4: 32.

(*b*) The Epistles give to the Church's unity a prominence that should be
carefully noted since they are written out of a situation in which divisions
between Christians have already appeared. There are no separate
denominations in the New Testament but there are differences that led
to breaches of fellowship and the Corinthian letters bring before us
the menace of divisions. Special attention should be given to 1 Cor. 12:
4–30; Eph. 4: 1–16. Both these passages make it plain that the Church is a
living organism, a body united to Christ its Head, each member dis-
charging its own function within the one fellowship.

The figures used in the Epistles to describe the Church again imply
its unity – the body of Christ, the bride of Christ, the household of God
(Cf. Eph. 2: 19; 1 Cor. 3: 16–17; 12: 12; 1 Pet. 2: 5, 9–10).

(*c*) In the Gospels attention should be drawn to the words spoken at the
Last Supper recorded by the three evangelists: This is my body. The
saying implies that at the Last Supper Jesus gave Himself to His disciples
so that they might become united to Him in the unity of His body (cf.
1 Cor. 10: 16).

(*d*) The teaching of St John's Gospel about unity is often cited. The figure
of the vine and the branches (15: 1 ff.) reminds us not only of the unity of

11

Christ and His disciples but that the life in which the disciples share is derived from Christ who makes them one. The greater part of the chapter underlines the fuller significance of the unity of Christ's disciples. In Chapter 17, we have brought before us the secret of the unity of Christ and God, which Christ prays may be imparted to His disciples.

(e) The Church of the New Testament is one, and its unity is not based on expediency or created by external organization. It is not a sociological unity like that of the family. It is the creation of God and in spite of the devastating consequences of the divisions that mar the history of the Church, nothing can destroy its unity.

(f) Further, its unity is related to its mission. If the Church is the Body of Christ, it must be one, for Christ is undivided. The body is both the expression of the will and the instrument of its purpose. Hence the Church can only express the nature of Christ and be the agent of His purpose for the world if it is itself one. St Paul writes: 'God was in Christ reconciling the world to Himself . . . and having committed to us the ministry of reconciliation' (2 Cor. 5 : 19). To exercise that ministry means that we are reconciled as Churches to each other on the basis of love, holiness and truth. Otherwise what we are will speak louder than what we say.

God wills the unity of His Church in order that it may be an effective instrument of His redemptive power in creating a new heaven and a new earth, a community in which divisions based on race, sex, religious bitterness, and economic status are done away and the one Christ is all in all.

2. The divisions of the Church, even if some at least seem to have been unavoidable, have resulted in a distorted understanding of Christian Truth. In our separation from each other we are prone to stress those elements in our Faith to which we believe we have been called to bear witness and each communion tends to live by a part and not the whole of the Christian Gospel. Hence its apprehension of Christian Truth as well as its spiritual life tends to become unbalanced. One of the results of the coming together of Churches in the World Council of Churches is the growing recognition of our need of each other in the interpretation of the Christian Faith in its fullness.

3. Our divisions have been and still are the source of great confusion in the Mission Field. The younger Churches are torn between a loyalty to parent Churches which are divided from each other and a determination to concentrate Christian forces in the face of the resurgence of non-Christian religions and a blatant materialism. It is not surprising that they have proved to be the pioneers in the quest of Christian unity, for the burden of divisions thrust upon them by the West is intolerable.

4. Many of the historic divisions have ceased to be relevant to our own situation as Churches. The differences between Anglicans and Methodists, for example, do not coincide with our ecclesiastical boundaries. On the contrary, they cut across them. It was significant that when the tercentenary of the great Ejectment of 1662 was celebrated, Anglicans and Free Churchmen declared from common platforms that a similar tragedy could not take place today. There was little indication of the beating of the Nonconformist drum. While the issues were not blurred, the primary note of the celebrations was the recovery of Christian unity. Again, is it conceivable that the Methodists of the eighteenth century would have felt obliged to leave the Church of England if that Church had the same concern for the salvation of this country as it manifests today? What are described as 'Methodist Doctrines' found a powerful exponent in the utterances of the late William Temple, particularly in his teaching about conversion, salvation by faith and the Holy Spirit. Clearly there are important differences in theological emphasis, ways of worship and social doctrine between Anglicans and Methodists. Increasingly, however, those differences overleap denominational barriers.

5. The need to concentrate Christian forces in this country is as urgent as it is overseas. Here as elsewhere the crucial conflict is not between the various historic Churches or between different schools of Christian thought but between a way of life that is centred in the revelation of God in Christ and a way of life that leaves God out of account altogether. To fail to discern the signs of times is to forfeit the claim and privilege of spiritual leadership. It is time the Churches realized where the battle for the Christian Gospel is joined. The things about which we differ as Churches are small compared with the things about which we agree over against the powerful onslaught made upon the Christian Faith and its values in modern society. The pressure of events is a pointer to duty for those who have eyes to see.

6. Our disunity means inefficiency. We are often told that we should not advocate Christian unity on the grounds of efficiency. Certainly the ultimate sanction is the nature of the Church as described in the New Testament. But efficiency is surely part of the fruit of the Spirit who orders all things for the doing of the divine will. Who can say today, as he surveys the life of the Churches in any town or village and takes account of the distribution of material resources and man-power, that the Churches are setting an example to the nation in efficiency? What a difference it would make if together in every area we could plan for Christian advance and use to the full our common resources! The gulf between the Churches and the vast majority of the people of this country presents a warning that we should heed without delay.

For discussion

1. Let the leader or somebody whom he may appoint give a short exposition of 1 Cor. 12 : 4–30 and Eph. 4 : 1–16, followed by discussion. Bring out particularly

(i) the relation of the Church and its members to Christ. Unity in a sense is a by-product of that relationship.

(ii) the relation between unity and mission, showing that unity and evangelization are not alternatives but indissolubly linked together.

2. Consider what we have lost as well as what we have gained by our divisions. Inquire how far these divisions are relevant today and how in a united Church they may be used for the fulfilment of God's purpose.

3. What do you consider to be the main conflict which Christianity has to face today? How far would the coming of a united Church in England promote the winning of England for Christ?

2. Theological Considerations
(*Report pp. 15–33*)

The conversations between the Church of England and the Methodist Church began not with the consideration of a 'scheme of reunion' but with certain issues of great theological importance. More time in the sessions was devoted to the theological basis of unity between our two Churches than to the particular proposals contained in the report. It was believed that if we could achieve a sufficient measure of agreement about the authority of the Bible, the nature of the Gospel, Church Order, the Ministry of Sacraments, the formulation of a scheme to secure closer relations would not prove insuperable.

Readers of the 'Report' will have read the chapter entitled 'A Dissentient View', of which a summary will be given later. It bears witness to the fact that there were four members of the Methodist delegation who dissented from the Report. While no doubt they would willingly subscribe to much that is found in the section about to be reviewed, they would wish to put differently, and perhaps to dissent from, certain views there expressed. In the course of group study, attention should be directed to the main objections raised in the 'Dissentient View' and the grounds on which they rest.

The Anglican signatories of the Report with eight Methodist signatories found in 'Theological Considerations' a fair statement of their own convictions even if they did not wish to subscribe to every expression used or sentiment expressed.

(i) *Scripture and Tradition* (Report pp. 15–19)

'There is much significance in the question put to ordinands in both our Churches, the inquiry whether they believe that "the Holy Scriptures contain sufficiently all doctrine required of necessity to eternal salvation, through faith in Jesus Christ" and whether in consequence they will "teach nothing as required of necessity to eternal salvation but that which they are persuaded may be concluded and proved by scripture" ' (Report pp. 15–16)

From these statements certain plain inferences may be drawn:

(*a*) There are certain doctrines which are essential to eternal salvation and they are contained in Scripture. What are those? They are summarized in the historic creeds and may be described as the Apostolic witness to salvation through faith in Jesus Christ, the final revelation of God. This witness is what we mean by the Apostolic tradition which comprises the content of the message of the Gospel received by the apostles directly from their Lord. The Apostles were eyewitnesses of the life, ministry,

15

death and resurrection of Jesus. Hence they stand in a unique relationship with Jesus and it is for that reason that it is claimed that the Apostolic tradition or interpretation of the Gospel is normative. That is, it is the standard by which later traditions must be tested. The authority of the Bible and that of tradition can never, therefore, be equated.

(*b*) There are doctrines and practices built up into the life, worship and teaching of the Church which are not explicitly contained in Scripture. Few would wish today to maintain that no teaching must be entertained which is not to be found in Scripture. To take this view is to regard the Scriptures as a residuum of the past rather than a living dynamic force thrusting the Church out into a wider and deeper understanding of the Gospel and its implications. In a word, it is to deny the continuous guidance of the Holy Spirit. To acknowledge, for instance, that the doctrine of the historic episcopate (to be considered later) is not to be found in the Scriptures is not to rule it out as a true part of Christian tradition subsequent to the age of the Apostles. Since, however, it is not explicitly contained in Scripture, it cannot be regarded as essential to salvation. Similarly, the Methodist form of Church government is not contained in Scripture. Like other forms of government that are to be found in the principal Churches of Christendom, it has to do with historical situations for which there is no parallel in the Apostolic age. But it may be fairly claimed that the ordering of Church life in Methodism rests on principles which may be traced to the New Testament. To borrow the well-known dictum of the late Canon Streeter, all the Christian Communions in the light of the New Testament 'get prizes' although, we may add, for different reasons.

(*c*) Some doctrines or traditions which have found a home in the Church are plainly repugnant to Scripture and cannot therefore be entertained. These 'traditions' stand condemned in the light of the Christian Tradition or Apostolic witness set forth in the New Testament. 'When the reformers attacked tradition, it was to oppose the customs of men which had intruded themselves into the Church and which were repugnant to Scripture. They refused to conceive of tradition as a separate source of divine revelation to be given equal authority with Holy Scripture. But they in no wise despised what they had received from the past and appealed confidently to the great creeds and doctors of the Church' (p. 17).

(*d*) 'Scripture and tradition ought not to be put over against one another' (p. 17). First, because Scripture itself is not a recital of certain historical events or a number of statements divinely dictated. Scripture records the interpretation of events by the people of God, or the Church, under the inspiration of the Holy Spirit. We read, for example, not simply that Christ died but that He died for our sins. This is the message that was given to the Church and handed down through the New Testament as well as through worship and personal life. The Cross and Resurrection became 'the living stream of the Church's life'. Hence the Scriptures, as

16

the Report observes, are 'part of the tradition itself written as they were in the Church, by the Church, for the Church' (p. 18).

Secondly, Scripture, traditions, individual conscience, the Church are not opposing camps. All are subject to the control of the Holy Spirit who illumines and guides the company of the faithful which is the Church.

The following questions should be considered:

1. What do you understand by the oft quoted phrase: the Bible is the Word of God? In what sense should every scheme for reunion be tested by reference to the Bible?

2. 'God has blessed His people despite their separation and our varying traditions are rich with His gifts' (p. 19). What are the traditions as expressed in doctrine, worship and discipline in Churches other than our own that we most covet? What are those that we dislike? And why?

(ii) *Gospel, Church Order and Ministry* (Report: Chapter 3)

I. *Gospel*

(*a*) The Gospel is good news about God proclaimed by God Himself through the person of His Son who is one with Him in being and purpose. It is good news about God and His power to transform man and the universe of which he is a part into His own image. It is a redemptive message and opens up a way whereby man can be delivered from his pride and self-complacency, his false ambitions and lust for power and attain the freedom that comes of self-knowledge and a complete commitment to the demands of Christ through faith in His unchanging love.

(*b*) The Gospel is not a new set of rules but a new life – life in Christ through whom all things are made. That is, Christ is the ultimate.

(*c*) Life in Christ, however, is corporate. To be in Christ is to be in the Church. It is to become a member of the Body of Christ and share in its service. It is true that Christian discipleship requires personal commitment and a man is thus thrown back upon himself. But what he is committed to is a life of fellowship in love and love means corporateness. If religion is what a man does with his solitariness, then Christianity ends it. No Christian does anything alone. He is in the Church or the Body of Christ, and as a member of that Body, he lives and dies.

(*d*) Those who are in Christ look beyond the Church to the world which is the object of God's redeeming love. Their mission is to communicate the good news of the Gospel of God and to prepare the way for a new heaven and a new earth, an order in which everything, spiritual and physical, is gathered up into the purpose of God unveiled once and for all in Christ.

II. *Church Order*

(*a*) The Church is the agent of the Gospel. As we have seen, the Gospel is concerned with God acting in Christ on this earth. Its message is not simply that God is love but that God who is love became flesh in Christ so that He could be seen and touched. Through the visible, tangible and familiar facts of life the nature of God was manifested.

While the Church cannot take the place of Christ, it is through the Church that Christ seeks to reach out to the world. Just as the Gospel became incarnate in Christ, so it must become incarnate in and through His Church. The Church is His body and its life must be so ordered as to be the visible expression and instrument of His Spirit.

(b) 'Order is not contrary to the Gospel; its function is to express the Gospel and to contribute to its fulfilment in life' (p. 21). The structure of any society – religious or secular – reveals its inner principles and the order of the Church is therefore a matter of great importance. It exists not only to express the Gospel but to foster the new life which the Gospel has brought to the world.

(c) The Gospel has clothed itself in history in different modes of worship, thought, preaching, ministry and discipline, but it has retained a certain uniformity amid all its varied expressions. While, for instance, there are varieties of theological interpretation no Church can be regarded as 'Catholic' which does not accept the doctrines embodied in the Apostles' and Nicene Creed. Again, there are varieties of sacramental worship but in the celebration of the sacraments of Baptism and Holy Communion there are certain elements which are universally regarded as indispensable. Further, the structure of the Church, it would be agreed, must be related to the Church of the New Testament and, while the way must be open for development, continuity with the Apostolic Church must be preserved.

III. *Ministry*

There is a sense in which it is true that in the New Testament what is stressed is not the Ministry but ministries in which all members of the Body must share. A closer reading of the New Testament, however, shows that we have there both the Apostolic Ministry, as a separated order in which the Church is focused, and ministries of various kinds. The Report rightly affirms (p. 22) that in the New Testament the separated ministry is 'given'. By that is meant that it is represented as part of the structure of the Church according to the will of God. Ministers in common with all who belong to the Church are servants but as the servants of Christ they have authority to act in His name for the good of His Church. Their authority comes from Him. It comes from Him through His Church but not from His Church alone.

A. The question of the nature of ordination arises here.

(i) A separated ministry is in accordance with the New Testament pattern and the subsequent development of the structure of the Church. Apart from such crucial considerations, it is difficult to see

18

how the functions assigned to the ministry could be discharged if it were not separated.

(ii) The minister is separated to preach the Gospel, to conduct worship, to administer the Sacraments, to care for souls within and without the Church and proclaim the Gospel of divine forgiveness and reconciliation.

(iii) Ordination to this ministry means that a man has a vocation thereto which the Church acting in the name of Christ has judged to be authentic. The Church as the agent of Christ bestows upon him the authority which is fitted for the fulfilment of the functions of his office. To inquire whether the difference between a minister and a layman is a difference in kind or degree is to engage in fruitless controversy. Both are the servants of Christ. The difference lies in the authority committed to the ministry by Christ acting in and through His Church. Ordination confers a commission and, we may believe, grace to fulfil its demands.

B. *Priesthood*

The main points about the nature of priesthood are clearly set out in the Report (p. 23 ff.):

(i) It is important to bear in mind that the Church is a corporate priesthood, and its priesthood is derived from Christ. When we speak of Christ as priest, we mean that He offered to God the one perfect sacrifice of obedience, that He is the one mediator between God and man and that He ever lives to make intercession for the world He died to redeem.

(ii) The Church shares in that priesthood by proclaiming in Word and Sacrament the redemptive sacrifice of Christ on the Cross, by offering in the name of Christ forgiveness to those who repent and by holding before God in intercessory prayer the needs of a sinful world.

(iii) All believers are priests since each has his own place in the worship and service of the Church, and each has the privilege of direct access to God and His forgiving love. The worship and ministry of the Church exist to assist the individual believer to enter into communion with God and share in the fulness of His grace.

(iv) The doctrine of the priesthood of all believers has nothing to do with prerogatives or with the right of any member of the Church to perform any function simply by reason of the fact that he is a member. In the Methodist Church, while the normal practice is for ordained ministers to administer the Sacrament of Holy Communion, Conference, which is the ultimate authority within Methodism, may grant a dispensation to those who are not ordained to fulfil this function where it can be shown that otherwise Holy Communion could not be observed with sufficient frequency. It is a desire to make

19

adequate provision for sacramental needs and not a belief in the inherent right of lay administration that lies behind this dispensation. In the Church of England the celebration of Holy Communion is reserved to those who have been ordained to the priesthood. Likewise the formal declaration of absolution is reserved to the priesthood. In the Methodist Church it is not a general practice for the formal absolution of sins to be pronounced. On the other hand, those who are authorized to preach the word – whether they be ministers or lay preachers – are commissioned in the name of Christ to proclaim forgiveness to those who sincerely repent of their sins. No Anglican priest exercises functions which a Methodist minister may not exercise within the Methodist Church.

(v) In all these actions, as the Report notes (p. 23), the minister or priest acts representatively. That is, he speaks in the name and on behalf of the priesthood of believers – the royal priesthood which is the Church.

C. *Episcopacy*

1. Methodists often ask why Anglicans attach so much importance to episcopacy. In the Interim Statement (pp. 25 ff.) the reasons are set out as positively as possible and may be here summarized.

(i) The episcopate is intended to symbolize and safeguard the apostolic mission and authority within the Church. Historically the episcopate became the organ of this mission and authority. The episcopate, in fact, is designed to preserve the apostolic witness.

(ii) The episcopate seeks to guard the Church against erroneous teaching.

(iii) The bishop represents the whole Church to the diocese and the diocese to the Church.

(iv) The bishop is the chief pastor of the flock.

(v) Since the bishop symbolizes the authority of the Apostles and the unity and continuity of the Church through the ages, he is the appropriate agent for the ordination of men to the ministry of the one, holy, catholic and apostolic Church.

2.

(i) On more than one occasion, Methodism has made it plain that there are certain interpretations of episcopacy which it could not accept. The declaration of Conference 1939, quoted in part in the Report (p. 12), should be studied. There it is stated that Conference could not accept episcopacy if such acceptance involved the admission that it is indispensable to the Church. It is further stated that 'it could not accept the theory of apostolic succession interpreted as the succession of bishops in the principal sees of Christendom . . . and regarded as constituting the true and only guarantee of sacramental grace and right doctrine'.

(ii) In any proposals for unity, Methodists would require that the same liberty of interpretation should prevail at the stage of full communion or organic unity as at present exists in the Church of England. This does not mean that Methodists should accept the fact without inquiring about the theology of episcopacy. It does mean that within agreed limits, in the event of closer relations with the Church of England, no single interpretation should be regarded as obligatory.

(iii) Methodism has distributed its episcopal functions among various officers including presidents and ex-presidents of Conference, chairmen of Districts, and Circuit superintendents. There is no surrender of principle if some of these functions are delegated to one office. But the episcopate is not to be viewed apart from the Church but must rather be integrated into its life with the ministry and the laity having their due place. The episcopate is thus historic not only in the sense that in the past it has assumed certain forms but that it is capable of future development as part of the structure of the Church.

(iv) The question is sometimes asked why it is that if many – perhaps most – Anglicans do not take the view that the episcopate is of the essence of the Church (so that where there are no bishops, there is no Church), there should be an insistence on the acceptance of episcopacy for inter-communion as well as organic unity. The answer is that the Church of England regards the episcopate for the reasons given above (C. 1, p. 20) as a precious inheritance which they cannot surrender. It believes, as Methodists do, that unity means not the abandonment of our inheritance but its preservation in a new and richer context.

(v) Methodism may find in the historic episcopate a confirmation of its own belief in the unity and continuity of the Church, the partnership between the generations in Christian history, the importance of pastoral care and the necessity of an Apostolic ministry.

Questions to be considered

1. How far is it true to say that apathy about Christian unity among Christians is often due to the conception of Christianity as a private or individualistic relation between man and God?

2. It is sometimes said that Church Order is of quite secondary importance and that it is the Gospel or Faith that matters. What do you think of this view?

3. Do you consider that it is possible for the Church to survive without a separated ministry? What is your view of ordination?

4. What do you believe to be the difference, if any, between 'a minister' and 'a priest'? If there is a difference, is it important?

5. Discuss the view that while episcopacy is not indispensable to the life of the Church, it is a precious heritage that should not be surrendered.

(iii) *The Sacraments* (Report pp. 28–33)

Attention is first drawn in the chapter on 'The Sacraments' (pp. 28–9) to the following points:

   (i) Both the Church of England and the Methodist Church hold that the sacraments of Baptism and Holy Communion are of divine appointment and perpetual obligation.

   (ii) The official orders of service for Baptism and Holy Communion in the two Churches present no difficulty. One of the two orders authorized for Holy Communion in the Methodist Church corresponds substantially with the Order of Holy Communion in the Book of Common Prayer.

   (iii) Certain usages in either Church will be unfamiliar and perhaps uncongenial to the other. The Methodist use of unfermented wine is likely to prove more difficult than either liturgical vesture or the disposal of the consecrated elements after Communion. It is, however, to be hoped that the use of unfermented wine will not prove a serious obstacle. While it is the general custom for fermented wine to be used in the Church of England, there is no rubric to the effect that unfermented wine is disallowed. There are indeed parishes where unfermented wine is the custom. This is one of the questions which should be discussed by Methodists and Anglicans in joint groups.

   (iv) Methodists who desire to consider the sacramental doctrine of the Church of England should consult Articles of Religion (XXV to XXXI), the Revised Catechism and the services in the Prayer Book.

   (v) There is no official statement of Methodist sacramental doctrine. Chapter 4 of the Report (pp. 29–33) contains a brief exposition of the theology of the Sacraments which may serve as a basis for discussion.

The following points should be noted in relation to the Sacraments:

   (*a*) The Sacraments of Baptism and Holy Communion are Sacraments of the Gospel. In both the Gospel of grace is proclaimed. They tell of what God has done for the redemption of the world.

   (*b*) Both our Churches are agreed that Baptism is of divine appointment. In the New Testament it is the normal rite of admission into the Christian Church.

   (*c*) On p. 30 there is a brief summary of the teaching of the New Testament about Baptism. The question arises as to the applicability of this teaching to Infant Baptism. Since, however, our Churches are not divided from each other on this issue, it does not call for immediate consideration.

(*d*) We need specially to bear in mind the concluding observations on Baptism in the Report (p. 31):

First, what makes the rite of baptism valid is what God has done in Christ.

Secondly, there must be a response of faith but in infant baptism the faith is that of the Church. What has been described as the complete baptismal event extends throughout the whole of life. In this connexion, confirmation or acceptance into Church membership plays a significant part. In confirmation through the power of the Holy Spirit we make our own the faith of the Church. The rite thus embodies an indispensable stage in spiritual growth. But it does not mark the first gift of the indwelling of the Holy Spirit.

Thirdly, Baptism means initiation into the Christian life. The baptized receives the status of a child of God within the family of the redeemed. In that sense, the child baptized is regenerate. He is set in an environment in which he can grow into the image of Christ.

Holy Communion

(i) In Holy Communion what Christ has done is of primary significance. At every Communion Christ Himself presides and offers Himself anew to us in His sacrificial love.

(ii) Holy Communion is an act of remembrance or recollection by which the great 'salvation' events in the life of our Lord are rehearsed. It is also an anticipation of what lies beyond history in the fulfilment of the divine purpose. There is a looking back and a looking forward to the gathering up of all things in Christ.

(iii) The act of remembrance leads to communion. By feeding upon Christ as He offers Himself to us, we become His body. His life pulsates through us.

(iv) We become, through partaking of common food, united to each other. The Church militant and triumphant unites in Holy Communion, and finds reconciliation through the Cross.

(v) The Sacrament of Holy Communion is a sacrifice. There is no question that the sacrifice of obedience which our Lord made on the Cross was offered once and for all. It cannot be repeated. By our remembrance and communion, however, we re-present it. As we offer ourselves to God in response to His sacrifice of obedience, we become united to Christ in His death. We share in His redemptive purpose and make a glad return to God of the new life which has been put into us.

Questions to be considered

1. What are your views about the use of fermented or unfermented wine at Communion? How can the problem presented by the different practices best be solved?

23

2. Discuss the statement on the Sacraments outlined above. Does it present difficulties? How far does it represent the thought of Methodists or Anglicans you know?

Note on 'open communion'

In many Methodist churches, it is customary for an invitation to be given to all who love the Lord Jesus Christ to communicate. The practice needs to be considered with some care not only with reference to reunion but to missionary work overseas.

1. It is commonly said that Methodism has never 'fenced' the Table. Historically there is no foundation for this statement. The Rev. John C. Bowmer has examined the evidence in his two volumes: *The Sacrament of the Lord's Supper* and *The Lord's Supper in Methodism 1791–1960* (Epworth Press). There is also a letter from him on the subject in the *Methodist Recorder*, 4 July 1963. In this letter Mr Bowmer shows that when Methodists founded their own Society (July 1740) they had to deal with the question of the admission of non-members to the Lord's Supper. It was agreed

(i) that care should be taken as to who was admitted into the Society, and,

(ii) that notes of admission to the Lord's Supper should be given to none but 'those who come to us on the days appointed in each quarter' (John Bennet's Minutes, 1745).

These notes, as Mr Bowmer points out, were not continued indefinitely in the case of any individual. The normal requirement was membership of Society.

2. The conception of the Lord's Supper as a converting ordinance was cherished by Wesley and his followers. There is no doubt that Wesley received earnest 'seekers' to Communion and did not restrict participation to the 'converted'. Earnest seekers, however, had already some measure of faith but it had not come alive in their own experience (Sermon XII on 'The means of Grace' often quoted in this connexion is directed against those within the Society who abstained from communicating). By conversion Wesley means the 'evangelical conversion' which he experienced in Aldersgate Street.

Wesley did not insist on confirmation as an indispensable condition of admission to communion. There was, in fact, a wide degree of laxity in regard to confirmation in the eighteenth century.

3. In official Wesleyan Methodism, until Methodist Union 1932, the attitude to 'open communion' is indicated in Simon's *Summary of Methodist Law and Discipline* pp. 39–40, 1923 edition (as quoted by Mr Bowmer, *The Lord's Supper in Methodism 1791–1960*): 'As regards strangers occasionally attending our services who desire to participate with us, they may be reasonably expected to assure the minister of their fitness by explaining to him that they are members of another Church or for what reason, not being members of any Church, they desire to be communicants; and such occasional cases can be met by the issue of a special note of admission by the minister. That the Table of the Lord should be open to all comers is surely a great discredit and a serious peril to any Church.'

In the Methodist New Connexion, notes of admission were expected of those who did not belong to the Society. The Bible Christian Conference in its Annual Letter 1824 urged the Society Stewards to take care whom they admitted and to see that the people produced their Class Tickets. The United Methodist Free Churches gave to each member a year's supply of sacramental tickets. In the United Methodist Church there is no reference in the Standing Orders to the showing of Class Tickets. The Primitive Methodist Church sought to control admission to the sacrament by requiring that each member or visitor belonging to any other community should show his ticket or note of admission (See *The Lord's Supper in Methodism 1791–1960*, pp. 34 ff.).

4. The practice of 'open communion' is partly the outcome of the dissociation of the Christian life from Church membership and its ordinances. Such dissociation is contrary to the teaching of the New Testament where to be a Christian is to be in the Church. Partly, however, it is the result of an unwillingness to repel anybody from the Lord's Table who wishes to partake and a desire to provide an opportunity for public commitment to Christ. Three points might here be discussed. First, to repel a person from the Lord's Table is one thing. To encourage those who are not members of any Church to come to the supreme rite of Christian worship without instruction as to its meaning and implications is another. According to the Deed of Union 1932, it is the duty and privilege of *members* of the Methodist Church to avail themselves of this Sacrament. Secondly, to love the Lord Jesus Christ carries with it the responsibility of Church membership. Neither the Sacrament of Baptism nor that of Holy Communion should be isolated from the life of the Church and the place in it of each member. Thirdly, the practice of open communion is out of harmony with the idea of the 'gathered Church' which is fundamental to the life of the Free Churches.

5. If by 'open communion' we mean that all members of the Church of Christ in good standing are welcome, let us hope that the practice will become universal without undue delay.

25

3. The Proposals
(*pp. 7–13*)

The proposals that are before the Church of England and the Methodist Church may now be summarized.

1. It is proposed that closer relations between the two Churches should be achieved in two stages.

(I) Full communion; by which is meant the freedom of the members of each Church in good standing to communicate in the other and of the ministers of each Church to preach and celebrate in the other if invited to do so.

(II) Organic union; by which is meant the bringing of the activities of both Churches into one body and under one constitution.

2. While the final goal of unity must be kept in view, the present proposals are specially concerned with 'full communion' as already defined.

Full communion will involve:

(*a*) An integration of ministries which implies the acceptance by the Methodist Church of Episcopacy in continuity with the historic episcopate and the practice of episcopal ordination for its ministers in the future.

(*b*) The appointment by the Methodist Conference of certain ministers to be consecrated bishops and the establishment of a parallel episcopate – Anglican and Methodist.

(*c*) The retention by each Church of its own life, worship and identity.

(*d*) The provision of means by which the Churches could co-operate by consultation, common action and common devotion at all levels.

(*e*) The coming together of the two Churches in a service of reconciliation to be followed in due course by the consecration of Methodist ministers to the episcopate.

3. The following order of events may be suggested:

1963–1965 Considerations of Report by various courts in the Church of England and the Methodist Church. Judgement of Quarterly meetings December 1964. Judgement of Synods May 1965.

1965 Submissions of report for judgement to the Convocations of Canterbury and York and the Methodist Conference. In the event of a favourable judgement, appointment of joint committee to consider (*a*) any amendments sent from Church courts, (*b*) constitutional changes involved in full communion and any necessary parliamentary legislation, (c) arrangements for services of reconciliation, (d) consultation about the situation in Scotland and Wales.

1966 Report of joint committee to Convocations and the Methodist Conference.

1967 New legislation to be considered by Methodist Synods regarding the appointment of Methodist bishops by the Methodist Conference, as well as the procedure proposed and the functions to be assigned to the bishops thus appointed.

1967 or 1968 Service of reconciliation – probably in London – to be followed by services of reconciliation throughout the country, so as to provide an opportunity for ministers and members in every area to participate. It would not be possible for the services to cover attendance of the total membership of each Church. Provision, however, would be made for the attendance of the ministers of both Churches and for an adequate representation of the laity.

4. The Service of Reconciliation
(*pp. 37–47*)

The following points should be noted:

1. The Declaration of Intention should be studied with care. The title of the service reminds us that what is proposed is not the absorption of one Church by the other but the coming together of two Churches on the basis of truth and love. Each Church declares that 'in the union of ministries neither of us wishes to call in question the reality and spiritual effectiveness of the ministry of the other Church' (p. 38). This declaration is of first importance for without it no progress towards closer relations can be made. Equally significant is the final paragraph (p. 38) in which there is expressed the resolve to pray that 'God will renew the gifts that He has given to us all and will enable each of us to enter into that which He has given to the other'.

2. The first act is of thanksgiving and penitence (p. 39). In offering thanksgiving it is fitting to remember, in addition to those who are acknowledged in the opening prayer, the pioneers of Christian unity, Edinburgh 1910, the World Council of Churches, the Church of South India, the United Church of Canada, Lord Fisher's Cambridge sermon as Archbishop of Canterbury, 1946, the labours and prayers of Pope John XXIII. The prayers of penitence like all prayers need to be sincere. There are many who disclaim responsibility for divisions within the Church. They tell us that as far as they are concerned they would welcome a united Church today. Why, then, should they repent?

It is true that we are not directly responsible for the historic divisions of the Church. And yet in different ways, often unrecognized by ourselves, we may be responsible for their perpetuation. We think of the presence of denominational pride, unexamined generalizations about other denominations, an unwillingness to be disturbed or to change our ways of thought and worship, a failure to appreciate traditions other than our own, a suspicion that assurances given by other Churches are not authentic, a lack of faith and confidence in the possibility of reconciliation – not to speak of 'non-theological motives' such as cultural and social differences which are based on bad theology.

3. In the service of reconciliation the lay membership of the one Church is received by the other. This is followed by the reception of the ministry of the one Church by the other. In regard to the latter act, there are certain observations to be made.

29

(*a*) It is the intention of the service that the fullness of the inheritance of the one Church should be communicated to the other and that both laity and ministry should receive such grace as is needful to fulfil their mission in the new fellowship which they now share.

(*b*) The bishop lays his hands on the head of each Methodist minister and the presiding Methodist minister lays his hands on the head of each bishop and priest.

Laying on of hands does not signify ordination in this service. The inference may not unnaturally be drawn that the laying on of hands means ordination, since normally the practice is found within Methodism only in connexion with ordination. It is, however, fitting that, since each Church desires to give to the other the gifts and blessings it has received through its own ministry, this physical act should be included. But we must not isolate it from the rest of the service. The preceding prayer in the case of the reception of the Methodist and Anglican ministers is of primary significance and it is ratified by the manual act. In the prayer preceding the laying on of hands on Methodist ministers we read: 'Renew thy blessings already given and upon thy servants do thou pour thy Holy Spirit to endue each according to his need with grace for the office of priest in the Church of God' (p. 43).

What the need of each is God alone fully knows and He alone can supply it.

The use of the word 'priest' should not be misconstrued. We may rest content with the Prayer Book interpretation which does not differ from what is understood by 'minister' in the Methodist Church. It is desirable that if the ministry of the one Church is to be received by the other, it should be in the form and phraseology that are traditionally employed in the Churches concerned. Hence when we come to the reception of bishops and priests in the Church of England by the Methodist Church, we read: 'Renew thy blessings already given and pour out thy Holy Spirit upon them for the work of a minister in thy Church' (p. 46).

No service is free from possible misconstruction. The laying on of hands should not be excluded because it is sometimes associated with a mechanical view of ordination which has few adherents. Nor, again, should it be excluded because it could be taken to imply that the service of reconciliation means ordination, or re-ordination. The service of reconciliation means fulfilment of existing ministries in the wider fellowship of two Churches in full communion with each other.

Note. The leader should explain the purpose of the service, show how it is built up and invite the views of the group upon it. To read the service aloud in the group is a practice to be commended.

5. Safeguards and Reassurances
(*pp. 48–50*)

1. The Methodist Church entered upon the conversations that have led to the publication of the 'Report' on the understanding that the same liberty of interpretation of the nature of Episcopacy and priesthood would be accorded to it when the two Churches are in full communion as at present prevails in the Church of England. Anglicans, for their part, are anxious that this understanding should be honoured. They desire, however, the assurance that once relations of full communion are established, episcopal ordination will be invariable in the Methodist Church.

2. Anglicans would also require that the celebration of the Eucharist should be confined to bishops and priests, and that the declaration of the absolution and remission of sins to penitent sinners should be acknowledged as part of the priestly and ministerial office.

At present in the Methodist Church lay administration of the Sacrament of Holy Communion is only authorized where there is insufficient provision for ministerial celebration.

In regard to confession and absolution, the hymns of Charles Wesley and the sermons of John Wesley and the historic discipline of Methodism as symbolized by the class meeting and evangelistic enterprise point to a recognition of the importance of the priestly office even if the terms 'priest' and 'priesthood' are not in the denominational vocabulary, except in relation to Christ and the Church. As the Report observes, the forgiveness of sins is central to the Methodist 'ethos' and the offer of forgiveness exercised by many ministries is an essential part of the pastoral office of the minister (p. 50).

3. The Methodist Church would require an assurance that relations of intercommunion and fellowship with non-episcopal Churches which it now enjoys should remain unimpaired. The same assurance would be required by the Church of England. The assurances apply to Stage I and Stage II. As far as the relations of Methodism with the other British Free Churches and the member Churches of World Methodism are concerned, there is every reason to suppose that in the interval between Stage I and Stage II changes in the relations of the Free Churches other than Methodism to the Church of England will have taken place. Similar changes may be anticipated in the relations between Methodists outside England and episcopal Churches in different areas. But existing relations of intercommunion and fellowship must be maintained. The difficulties may be faced if and when they arise.

4. It is reasonable to require that the domestic discipline of one Church should be respected by the other. An Anglican who for some reason is debarred from taking Communion in the Church of England should not be admitted to Communion in the Methodist Church. Confirmation in the Church of England is the normal requirement for admission to Communion. Hence 'unconfirmed Anglicans' should not be admitted to Communion in the Methodist Church (p. 49). Another example is that of marriage discipline, and where two Churches are in full communion, it is fitting that the marriage discipline of either Church should be respected by the other.

Questions for Study

1. Consider the importance of confession and absolution, and the ways by which the need for both have been met in the Methodist Church and the Church of England.

2. What special difficulties could arise in the relations between Methodism and other non-episcopal Churches if there were full communion between the Methodist Church and the Church of England?

3. Discuss the desirability of each Church respecting the domestic discipline of the other in relation to

(*a*) Holy Communion.
(*b*) Marriage.

6. Some Practical Problems
(*pp. 51–55*)

It is obvious that certain practical problems will face both communions if full communion is achieved. They cannot be explored in any detail at present but it is inevitable that questions as to subsequent developments will arise in the minds of many members of both Churches.

There were substantial reasons why the quest for unity was conceived in two stages. Among them reference may be made to tensions in the Church of England and the Methodist Church and the difficulties involved in the present form of establishment which could not be resolved without prolonged legal processes. There is little opposition in Methodism to the official recognition of the Church by the State and there are many Methodists who share the view that the withdrawal of such recognition at the present time would seriously weaken the moral and spiritual fabric of the nation. If, however, organic union were under consideration, Methodism would desire a form of establishment that was consistent with the spiritual freedom of the Church.

On the other hand, Stage I by itself is not an adequate expression of Christian unity. The Sacrament of Holy Communion must not be isolated from the wider fellowship of the Church. To meet together at the Holy Table and then maintain our separate ways in Christian witness and fellowship in thought and prayer is to exchange one scandal for another. It is a scandal that we cannot unite at the Lord's Table. It would be a scandal if having met there we refused to advance to fuller unity.

2. Details of a scheme of organic unity which may not mature for 15–20 years cannot now be given. It would be idle to attempt a blueprint of the constitution of an organically united Church at the present time. Nevertheless in assenting to Stage I (full communion) we are assenting to Stage II (organic union) not in the sense that we are accepting a scheme of union in blind faith but that we are committing ourselves to seek the fullest possible visible unity that may be within the will of God for His Church.

A distinction must be drawn between the principle of organic union and a particular scheme of organic union. At no point shall we be manœuvred into a position of being virtually compelled to accept a particular scheme of organic union because we have assented to the principle of organic unity.

During Stage I there will be opportunities to discuss our joint pastoral, liturgical and social concerns and to prepare the way for a conception of a united Church which embodies the message, mission, unity and variety of the community of the people of God.

3. Questions arise about the changes that are to be anticipated during the period of full communion. While the two Churches will remain distinct, it is desirable that a body composed of representatives from both Churches should be set up to facilitate co-operation. There should be joint commissions, for example, on worship and training for the ministry with the possible establishment of united theological colleges. Problems connected with Anglican and Methodist training colleges for teachers and schools should be regarded as a common concern. In new areas there should be fuller consultation before churches are erected so as to avoid overlapping. Wherever possible both Churches should unite in communicating the Gospel to those without the Church by different types of missions, particularly teaching missions, and by establishing contact with industry.

If intercommunion leads to co-ordinated activities of this kind, it will pave the way to organic union. It will in fact become the inspiration and culmination of our united witness to the Christian Faith.

4. During Stage I there are certain practical problems for Methodists which will have to be faced. They are noted in the Report, p. 53. A few examples may be given:

(a) The acceptance of episcopacy should not impair the authority of Conference, either in its representative or ministerial sessions. Methodist bishops would be responsible to Conference as well as appointed by Conference. Candidates for ordination would be presented by bishops to the ministerial session on the advice of examining bodies such as now function. Matters of ministerial discipline would be presented by bishops to this session.

(b) It is important again that the work of the departments which are an integral element in the Methodist constitution should not be affected if episcopacy is adopted. The activities of the District are presented to Conference through the departments and Conference is represented to the districts by the departments. The relationship of the departments to an episcopal ministry will therefore need careful study.

(c) The relation of the Anglican and Methodist bishop is another question that arises. During Stage I, as already indicated, there will be parallel episcopates and the authority of each bishop will be confined to his own diocese or district. But there will be opportunities for joint consultation.

(d) The position of the Methodist layman will remain unchanged during Stage I, except for the fact that the need for the lay administration of Holy Communion will disappear. But, as the Report affirms, 'local preachers and class leaders will still exercise their gifts as widely as they do now'.

Questions for Study

1. Why is it considered important that Stage I should lead to Stage II? There is intercommunion between the Free Churches but it has not led to organic union. What explanation have you to suggest?

2. What kind of a constitution would you suggest for a united Church if organic union were proposed for immediate consideration?
3. What, as far as you can see, are the practical problems likely to arise in Stage I (*a*) for Anglicans (*b*) for Methodists?

7.   A Dissentient View

(*pp. 57–62*)

1. The writers of this chapter in the Report, while desiring the unity of the Church, which, they hold, need mean neither uniformity nor unity of organization, do not believe that it is to be found in a scheme which may prove divisive and 'though well-intentioned, is in principle sectarian and exclusive'. *i.e. will lead to further splits*

2. Turning first to the Section of the Report on *Scripture and Tradition*, they consider that it fails to recognize the normative place of Scripture or set out satisfactorily its relation to tradition.

Traditions which all Churches have must be constantly sifted by Scripture. But tradition represents 'the worldliness of the Church, Scripture points it to its supernatural origin and basis'.

3. *Episcopacy i.e. the rule of Bishops*

While Methodism has episcopacy in the scriptural sense of the word, it is clear from the Report that the only kind of episcopacy that will enable Methodism to have full communion with the Church of England is the historic episcopate. A united Church demands ordination within the historic episcopate. But, it is argued, the historic episcopate is incapable of proof, it has failed to safeguard doctrine, the possession of the authentic historic ministry by the Church of England is denied by Rome and, what is more important, the historic episcopate is without support in the New Testament. It is, indeed, inconsistent with the New Testament doctrine that the Church depends wholly upon God's gracious election, grasped by faith alone.

4. The act of the laying on of hands on the head of each minister is 'capable of being and in some quarters will be interpreted as an act of ordination'. There is ground for this since it has been explicitly stated that Methodism, however rich its heritage may be, cannot confer that gift which is conferred only by ordination within the historic succession. That Methodists lay hands on Anglicans is a brotherly and charitable gesture but it does not affect the issue. Methodists have no right to lay hands on Anglicans. If in fact there was a desire to prove that ordination was not implied, then neither party should lay hands on the other.

5. *Priesthood*

The term 'priest' in the Report is expressly connected with sacrificial

37

Communion

views of the Eucharist and with the power to pronounce absolution. The Statement in the Deed of Union that ministers hold no priesthood differing in kind from that which is common to the Lord's people should be recalled in the light of the doctrine of priesthood which the Church of England, as is made clear in the Report, is resolved to safeguard.

Sacraments

1. As a matter of principle, the Methodist Church is right in allowing the possibility of lay celebration of Communion.

2. Some disquiet may be felt over the doctrines of baptismal regeneration and eucharistic sacrifice in the Report.

3. The stipulation made by the Methodist Church when it entered the 'conversations' that relations with non-episcopal Churches should remain unimpaired in the event of closer relations with the Church of England can be met only for Stage I. In view of the fact that in Stage II, Methodism will exist as part of a Church that has episcopal ordination as its invariable rule, it is improbable that it will be in communion with non-episcopal Churches.

Conclusion *Summing up the dissentient views*

It is hard to avoid the conclusion that the unification contemplated would mean the absorption of the Methodist Church by the Church of England. 'The more scriptural Church Order would be swallowed up by the less.' To move from a Church committed to the evangelical faith into a heterogeneous body permitting, and even encouraging, unevangelical doctrines and practices, would be a step backward which not even the desirability of closer relations could justify.

Other dissentient views in "What of the Conversations" M. R. F.

Questions to be considered

1. Examine the view that tradition represents 'the worldliness of the Church'.

2. Discuss the conception of unity underlying this chapter.

3. Do you think that acceptance of the historic episcopate as the basis of unity is a step backward and not a step forward in Church relations? In particular, consider the statement that 'the belief that the full and true being of the Church is dependent upon its possession of historic episcopacy is inconsistent with the New Testament doctrine that the existence of the people of God depends wholly upon God's gracious election, grasped by faith only' (p. 59).

4. Does the acceptance of the historic episcopate necessarily involve the doctrine of Apostolic Succession? If so, in what sense?

8.   Suggestions about Prayer for Unity

1. Prayer and study go together. It is easy to leave prayer out and harbour the illusion that prayer is simply honest thought or loving service. Prayer is waiting upon God to learn His will and to receive strength to do it. The reality of prayer is tested by the integrity and charity of our thought and actions.

2. Opportunities are offered for private prayer in daily devotions, in Sunday worship and particularly at Holy Communion. It is good to slip into a church of another communion on a week-day and offer a brief prayer for its peace and for the unity of the whole Church.

3. In groups, time should be allotted to prayer. From time to time there might be a period in which after a reading and a brief prayer by the leader, opportunity is given for free prayer. Two or three sentences spontaneously uttered by members of a group can greatly enrich the fellowship of prayer.

It is hoped that there will be joint discussion betweens Anglicans and Methodists in the coming months as well as meetings of the two Churches in separate groups. Such united groups should make provision for prayer as well as for discussion.

3. The following form of prayer is intended simply as a guide

Worthy of praise from every mouth,
of confession from every tongue,
of worship from every creature,
is thy glorious Name, O Father, Son, and Holy Ghost:
who didst create the world in thy grace
and by thy compassion didst save the world.
To thy majesty, O God, ten thousand time ten thousand
bow down and adore
Singing and praising without ceasing and saying
Holy, Holy, Holy, Lord God of hosts;
Heaven and earth are full of thy praises;
      Hosanna in the highest.

Nestorian Liturgy (shortened)
Daily Prayers, Penguin Books.

Reading

Psalm 122
1 Corinthians 12:4–11 or 12:27–13:13 or Ephesians 4:1–16

Prayers

Penitence.

Our shallowness in our relations with others
Our unwillingness to examine ourselves
Our want of faith, our wavering and fear
Our pride and prejudices so often confused with principles
Our hidden sectarianism and stubbornness
Our acquiescence in divisions that hinder the progress of the Gospel
O Lord, forgive.

Thanksgiving.

For thine infinite wisdom and love
For the revelation of thyself in Jesus Christ,
    God of God, Light of Light,
    who for us men and for our salvation shared our nature,
    lived and died and rose again
For the Holy Spirit, the Lord, the Giver of Life
For the Holy Catholic Church, the fellowship of the redeemed,
    the communion of saints
For the worship of the Church in word and sacrament
For the hope of eternal life
For those who have toiled in the cause of unity
For the work of the World Council of Churches
For the measure of unity already achieved between the Churches
    and the promise of fuller unity
For the communions we represent and the inheritance into which we
    have entered
For the vision of a Church united by thy grace in all its activities
    and equipped to fulfil its mission in the world
We thank thee, O God.
Bless the Lord, O my soul, and forget not all his benefits.

Petition and Intercession

This is our prayer:
That our love may grow ever richer in knowledge and insight of
    every kind
That our conduct may be worthy of the Gospel of Christ

That we may stand firm, one in spirit, one in mind, contending as one
man for the gospel faith [NEB with slight changes]

That we may remember the sheep that are not of the fold, seek out
the lost and proclaim the forgiveness of sins to the penitent and
show compassion to all mankind

That we may set forth thy righteousness in the life of society and in the
relations between nations

That we may by our example lead the world into the ways of reconciliation and peace.

Concluding Prayer

O Eternal God, the Father of spirits and the Lover of souls who didst
send thy Holy Spirit upon thy Church on the day of Pentecost, and
hast promised that he shall abide with it for ever, let that same Spirit
lead us into all truth, defend us from all sin, enrich us with his gifts,
refresh us with his comfort, rule our hearts in all things and lead us
in the way everlasting; through Jesus Christ our Lord, who with thee
and the same Spirit, liveth and reigneth one God, world without end.
Amen.

Benediction

9. Books

The following will prove helpful for the leader and members of the groups, particularly the first two publications:

An Interim Statement (S.P.C.K. and Epworth)
Anglicans and Methodists Talk Together (S.P.C.K. and Epworth)
S. C. Neill. *Anglicanism* (Pelican)
A. T. Hanson. *The Meaning of Unity* (Highway Press)
J. W. C. Wand. *The Church Today* (Pelican)
R. E. Davies. *Methodism* (Epworth and Penguin)
        The Bible and Unity (British Council of Churches)
E. W. Baker. *The Faith of a Methodist* (Epworth)
D. L. Edwards. *This Church of England* (S.C.M.)
The Unity We Seek. (Pamphlets published by the British Council of Churches)
R. Herbert. *Introducing Anglican Beliefs* (C.I.O.)
J. Banks. *A People Prepared: the Methodist Way in Faith, History and Practice* (Epworth)
S. C. Neill and others. *The Ministry of the Church* (Canterbury Press)
B. L. Manning. *The Hymns of Wesley and Watts* (Epworth)
H. Martin (ed.). *The Holy Communion* (S.C.M.)
R. N. Flew. *The Nature of the Christian Church according to the teaching of the Methodists* (Epworth)
E. H. Patey. *Anglicans and Methodists. A Study Guide.* (C.I.O. and Epworth)
D. L. Edwards. *This Church of England* (C.I.O.)